# ABOUT THIS BOOK

This book is designed for use by parents, caregivers, counselors, social service staff and protective investigators and can be read to children to help enable discussions about safe touching and sexual abuse. It is a storybook to help boys and girls, of different races and ethnic backgrounds learn about protecting their bodies, self-respect and how to assertively say "No" and "Don't touch me!" to anyone who touches them inappropriately. It includes open-ended questions following each lesson to encourage children to open up and explore their thoughts and feelings about safe touching, personal choices and when to seek others for help.

The book also introduces the topic of sexual abuse and ways to keep one's body private. It helps adults and children talk about sexual abuse together in a way which minimizes embarrassment and fear, but emphasizes self-protection and open communication. Children learn that it's OK to tell and talk about their feelings, and that sexual abuse is never their fault in hopes that they can continue to heal. Although sensitive, My Private Parts are Private! uses vivid and imaginative illustrations to build rapport and encourage adults and children to laugh, giggle and share. Each topic includes a keyword, simple explanation, open-ended question as well as a fun "Can you spot it                         engaged and help refocus them if they become distracted, anxious o                         being discussed.

# Nice to meet You!

Hi, my name is Dakota. I like to play with my friends at P.E., color with markers, ride my scooter and eat lots of candy.

· · · · · · · · · · · · · · · · · · · · · · · · · · · · · · · · · · · · · · · · · · · · · · · · · · · · · · · · · · · · · · · ·

What are your favorite things to do?

Can you spot it? |

3

# I am strong!

Some of the things that I like about myself are that I am smart, funny, good at basketball, and I like to help people.

· · · · · · · · · · · · · · · · · · · · · · · · · · · · · · · · · · · · · · · · · · · · · · · · · · · · · · ·

What are all of the things that you like about yourself?

Can you spot it? |

# It's My Body!

This is my body and some of the parts of my body are private.

· · · · · · · · · · · · · · · · · · · · · · · · · · · · · · · · · · · · · · · · · · · · · · · · ·

Can you point to the parts of my body that are private?  Now point to the parts of your body that are private.

Can you spot it?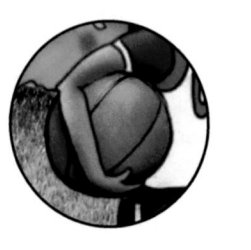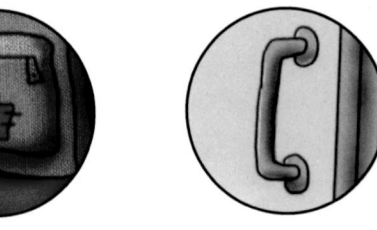

# Special People I Trust

Only special people that I trust are allowed to look at or touch my private parts.

· · · · · · · · · · · · · · · · · · · · · · · · · · · · · · · · · · · · · · · · · · · · · · · · · · · ·

Name all of the special people that are allowed to look at or touch your private parts?

Can you spot it?

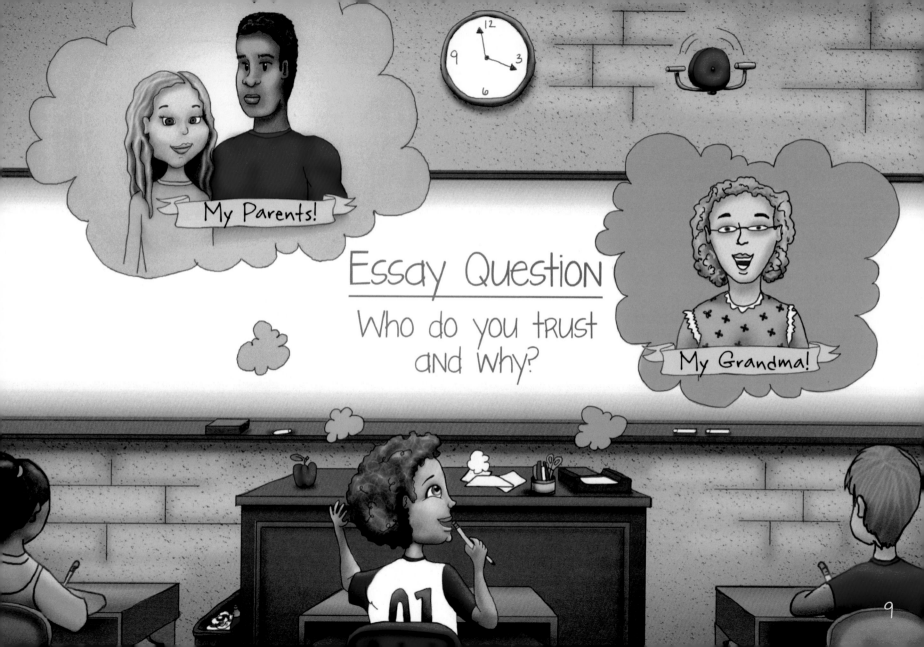

# Safe Touching

Some parts of my body are not private and other people are allowed to touch them if I want them to. For example, I like to give my friends at school High 5's.

. . . . . . . . . . . . . . . . . . . . . . . . . . . . . . . . . . . . . . . . . . . . . . . . . . . . . . . . . . . . . . . . . . .

Show me all of the safe touches you know of?

Can you spot it?

Even my best friends, teachers and some of my family are not allowed to look at or touch my private parts.

· · · · · · · · · · · · · · · · · · · · · · · · · · · · · · · · · · · · · · · · · · · · · · · · · · ·

Who are some of the people that are NOT allowed to look at or touch your private parts?

Can you spot it? |

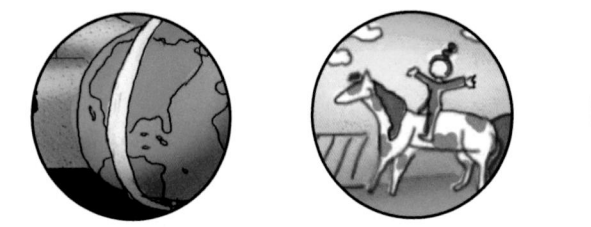

# My Choice!

It's NOT OK for someone to touch my private parts if I don't want them to and I HAVE A CHOICE about who touches my private parts.

. . . . . . . . . . . . . . . . . . . . . . . . . . . . . . . . . . . . . . . . . . . . . . . . . . . . . . . . .

How come it's NOT OK for others to touch your private parts?

Can you spot it?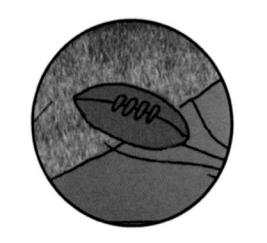

# Don't Touch Me!

It's OK to tell someone "No!" and "Don't touch me!" if they try to touch my private parts or if I feel uncomfortable when they touch me.

..................................................................

Let me hear how you would say "No" and "Don't touch me" to someone who tries to touch your private parts.

Can you spot it? |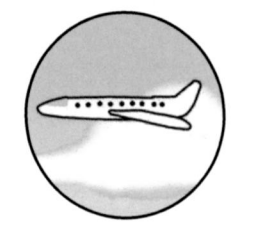

# No Secrets

It's important to tell someone I trust if anyone ever tries to touch my private parts.

It's OK to tell on anyone who tries to touch my private parts . . . even if they tell me it's a game, give me a gift, tell me to keep it a secret or say I will get in trouble if I tell on them.

· · · · · · · · · · · · · · · · · · · · · · · · · · · · · · · · · · · · · · · · · · · · · · · · · · · · ·

Name people that you trust and can tell if someone tries to touch your private parts.

Can you spot it? |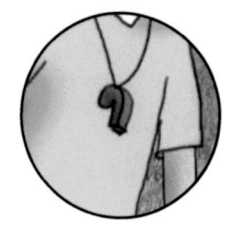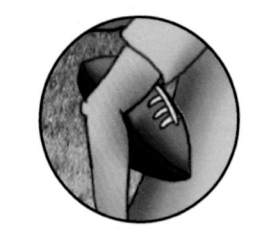

# Honesty is the Best Policy

I learned it's important to ALWAYS tell the truth when talking about my private parts. Keeping secrets about private parts is not OK.

...........................................................................

Give an example of a truth. How come it's important to tell the truth and not keep secrets about your private parts?

Can you spot it? |

When I was younger someone touched my private parts when they were not supposed to. But . . . that was before I learned some of the things in this book.

. . . . . . . . . . . . . . . . . . . . . . . . . . . . . . . . . . . . . . . . . . . . . . . . . . . .

Name all the people who have looked at or touched your private parts.

What do you think about someone who touches other people's private parts?

Can you spot it? |

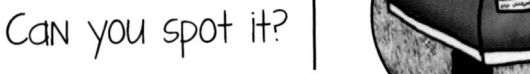

# Lots of Feelings

After they touched my private parts I thought about a lot of different things.  I also had a lot of different feelings inside.

. . . . . . . . . . . . . . . . . . . . . . . . . . . . . . . . . . . . . . . . . . . . . . . . . . . . . . . . .

What would you think and how would you feel if someone touched your private parts?

# It Wasn't My Fault!

Recently I talked with my parents and a counselor about my body and private parts. It was OK to talk to them about what happened to me. Although I was nervous, I felt much better after I talked to them. I learned it was not my fault and I am not a bad person just because someone touched my private parts when I did not want them to.

. . . . . . . . . . . . . . . . . . . . . . . . . . . . . . . . . . . . . . . . . . . . . . . . . . . . . . . . . . . . . . . . . . . . . . . . . . . . . . . . . . . . . .

What would you do if someone touched or tried to touch your private parts?

Can you spot it? │

# Let's Review!

- What are your favorite things to do?

- What are all of the things that you like about yourself?

- Can you point to the parts of your body that are private?

- Name all of the special people that are allowed to look at or touch your private parts?

- Show me all of the safe touches you know of?

- Who are some of the people that are NOT allowed to look at or touch your private parts?

- How come it's not OK for others to touch your private parts?

- Let me hear how you would say "No" and "Don't touch me" to someone who tries to touch your private parts.

- Name people that you trust and can tell if someone tries to touch your private parts

- Give an example of a truth..

- What do you think about someone who touches other people's private parts?

- What would you think and how would you feel if someone touched your private parts.

- What would you do if someone touched or tried to touch your private parts?

## About the Author

Robert Edelman, Ed.S. is the CEO of the Village Counseling Center (VCC) in Gainesville, Florida. He graduated from the University of Florida and is a Licensed Mental Health Counselor. Robert is the Founder of the Sexual Abuse Prevention and Treatment Program which has provided specialized evaluations and treatment for over a thousand children and adolescents with sexual abuse and/or sexual behavior problems. Robert was the founder and Co-Chair of the Child-on-Child Sexual Abuse Prevention Task Force and was an appointed member of the Gabriel Myers Work Group established by DCF to investigate issues related to Child-on-Child Sexual Abuse in Florida. He was also an invited member of the Child-on-Child Sexual Abuse and Children with Sexual Behavior Problems Strategic Planning Committee for the Office of Family Safety in Florida. Robert has presented trainings and seminars nationally on topics related to sexual development, sexual abuse prevention, trauma, child-on-child sexual abuse and youth with sexual behavior problems. Robert grew up in Miami Beach, Florida before attending U.F. where he met his wife Pebbles who has also dedicated her life to helping children and families. Robert and Pebbles still reside in Gainesville, Florida with their children Sophie and Jude.

## About the Illustrator

Graphic designer and Art Director by trade, Selena Carter, has put her talents to use in an array of fields. She works for clients across the country from her residence in Gainseville, FL. When she's not creating work to help spread good messages, she is spending time raising her four month old daughter, Ivey, who made her illustration debut on page 7.

# THANKS AND DEDICATION

Thanks to everyone at the Village Counseling Center for your amazing skills, humor and dedication towards helping children and their families. Special thanks to Paula Weaver for your loyalty, ethics and hard work all of these years. Just as important, thanks to the clients at VCC for your strength, resilience and willingness to overcome obstacles that most people never even realize.

Thanks to Magistrate Nancy Wilkov, Edith Jordan, Dr. Paul Wheeler, Dr. Marshall Knudson and Dr. Linda Abeles for all of the lessons you have taught me and for always being an inspiration. Thanks also to all of the staff at DJJ, DCF, Partnership for Strong Families and other Social Service Staff for the countless hours and energy you dedicate to helping the world be a better place for children. Never give up and always know that you do make a difference.

Thanks to Selena for the amazing illustrations and for being so easy to work with.

Special thanks to my sister, Melissa and parents, Harry and Sandy Edelman. I love and miss you every day.

Very special thanks to my wife, Pebbles for all of your love and beauty and for putting up with me for all of these years. I love you more than words on this paper could ever express.

This book is dedicated to the late Dr. Ted Shaw for his mentoring, trust and support. I also dedicate it to Vada Edleman ("Remember I love you") and my children, Sophie and Jude who inspire me to be the best I can be while sacrificing and allowing me to help others.

Made in the USA
Middletown, DE
19 October 2017